A GUIDE TO FRENCH GRAMMAR
Second Edition

Stanley Prince

Drawings by
Richard Walker

PACKARD PUBLISHING LIMITED
CHICHESTER

A GUIDE TO FRENCH GRAMMAR
Second edition

© Stanley R. Prince

This revised edition published in 1991 by Packard
Publishing Limited, Forum House, Stirling Road,
Chichester, West Sussex PO19 2EN.

Reprinted with amendments September 1992.

The first edition was published in 1975 by Henry E. Walter.

ISBN 1 85341 045 4

A CIP cataloguing record of this book is available from the
British Library.

Typeset by Barbara James, Deanlane End, Rowlands
Castle, Hampshire.
Printed and bound by Downland Reprographics,
Chichester, West Sussex.

PART G

15 JUST FOR FUN

15.1 Tongue Twisters

(1) Didon dîna, dit-on, de dix dodus dos de dix dodus dindons.

(2) Un chasseur sachant chasser doit savoir chasser sans son chien.

(3) C'est combien ces six cent six saucissons-ci? C'est six cent six sous ces six cent six saucissons-ci.

(4) Si six scies scient six cyprès, six cent six scies scient six cent six cyprès.

(5) Le vers est: le ver vert va vers le verre vert et vertical.

15.2 Conundrum

Q. Pourquoi ne faut-il pas trop nourrir un nain?

A   Parce qu'on risque d'en faire un ingrat (nain gras).

15.3 Quick Quiz

(1) Find a six letter French word containing all five vowels.

(2) Find two French words where the letter 'q' is not followed by the letter 'u'.

(3) Find two basic French words which can be pronounced in three different ways.

(4) Find a French word which contains a 'c' pronounced as a 'g'.

(5) Find a French word which changes completely in the plural.

(6) Find a French word beginning with a vowel, which is preceded by le and not l'.

(7) Find a French word containing the letter 'e' three times in a row.

Answers to Quiz at back of book (see page 57)

PART H

16 SUPPLEMENT

The Passé simple is included in this book for recognition purposes, since A-level students may well have access to a more literary type of French, where they would meet this tense.

The Past Anterior, and the Present Tense of the Subjunctive Mood, are likewise included for completeness, in order to assist students who take the subject beyond the confines of Common Entrance and GCSE.

16.1 Past Historic Tense (le passé simple)

(1)   The *past historic* is sometimes called the *past definite, preterite* or *aorist.*

(2)   It is a *simple* past tense, i.e. it has only one part, whereas the *perfect tense* has two.

(3)   Its use is confined to written French, i.e. literature of all kinds.

(4)   It is equivalent to the English *I went (J'allai),* but not *I have gone* which must be translated as *(Je suis allé).*

Formation

Regular Verbs + *aller*

A group	I group	
Donner *(er)*	Finir *(ir)*	Vendre *(re)*
Je donn*ai* – *I gave*	Je fin*is* – *I finished*	Je vend*is* – *I sold*
Tu donn*as*	Tu fin*is*	Tu vend*is*
Il donn*a*	Il fin*it*	Il vend*it*
Nous donn*âmes*	Nous fin*îmes*	Nous vend*îmes*
Vous donn*âtes*	Vous fin*îtes*	Vous vend*îtes*
Ils donn*èrent*	Ils fin*irent*	Ils vend*irent*

N.B.   Care must be taken with regular *-IR* verbs in the singular because *Je finis = I am finishing* (present), and *I finished* (past).

CONTENTS

FOREWORD TO THE SECOND EDITION

This new edition has afforded me the opportunity, both to redraft the original text and add to its content. Sections covering verbs requiring *à* or *de*, and the passive voice, have been included for completeness, whilst the listing of prepositional phrases and *faux-amis* stems from an awareness of how such information has helped my own pupils to avoid linguistic pitfalls, as well as from my personal fascination with the vagaries of language, which I hope to share with my readers. The inclusion of cartoons, tongue twisters, a conundrum and a quiz are further innovations which should provide some welcome relief from the inevitably more serious process of learning.

The main aim, however, remains unchanged. It is to provide pupils with easy access to all the information required for revision at a glance, and I have endeavoured to produce a handy reference book of key facts and grammatical rules, as well as guides to the tackling of comprehension work and essay writing. The contents provide a full survey of traditional grammatical points, and should be an ideal way to consolidate, revise or check for gaps in one's knowledge. Whilst not taking the slightest issue with the current emphasis on communication skills, it is becoming increasingly recognized that language is not always best learned simply by a form of osmosis, and that some sort of mental application is probably required if real mastery is to be achieved. Thus, my book may well be viewed as a formal back-up to much of the 'softer' illustrative material currently on offer.

Finally, I should like to acknowledge the encouragement I have received from my new publisher and from pupils both past and present. It is gratifying to learn that the first edition of my book was used by students not only at Common Entrance, GCE and GCSE levels but also at 'A' level and beyond. Good luck with this new edition and happy reading!

S.R.P.
Chichester, 1991

PART A

GRAMMAR

1 VERBS

1.1 Present Tense (le présent)

Regular Verbs

Donner – **to give**

Je donne	I give, I am giving
Tu donnes	You give, you are giving
Il donne	He gives, he is giving
Elle donne	She gives, she is giving
Nous donnons	We give, we are giving
Vous donnez	You give, you are giving
Ils donnent	They give, they are giving (m)
Elles donnent	They give, they are giving (f)

Finir –	**to finish**	**Vendre** –	**to sell**
Je finis	I finish, etc.	Je vends	I sell, etc.
Tu finis	You finish	Tu vends	You sell
Il finit	He finishes	Il vend	He sells
Elle finit	She finishes	Elle vend	She sells
Nous finissons	We finish	Nous vendons	We sell
Vous finissez	You finish	Vous vendez	You sell
Ils finissent	They finish (m)	Ils vendent	They sell (m)
Elles finissent	They finish (f)	Elles vendent	They sell (f)

Four Important Irregular Verbs

Être	–	to be	Avoir	–	to have
Je suis		I am	J'ai		I have
Tu es		You are	Tu as		You have
Il est		He is	Il a		He has
Elle est		She is	Elle a		She has
Nous sommes		We are	Nous avons		We have
Vous êtes		You are	Vous avez		You have
Ils sont		They are (m)	Ils ont		They have (m)
Elles sont		They are (f)	Elles ont		They have (f)

Aller	–	to go	Faire	–	to do, to make
Je vais		I go	Je fais		I do
Tu vas		You go	Tu fais		You do
Il va		He goes	Il fait		He does
Elle va		She goes	Elle fait		She does
Nous allons		We go	Nous faisons		We do
Vous allez		You go	Vous faites		You do
Ils vont		They go (m)	Ils font		They do (m)
Elles vont		They go (f)	Elles font		They do (f)

N.B. (1) These are the only four verbs which end in *-ont.* All others end in a silent *-ent* in 3rd person plural.

       (2) Care! *Vous êtes; Vous faites.* Also *Vous dites.* All others end in *-ez* in 2nd person plural.

Irregular -ER Verbs

N.B. (1) *Aller* is the only completely irregular verb.

       (2) *Appeler* and *jeter* double the final consonant

       (3) *Acheter, lever, mener* take a grave accent   in sing. and

       (4) *Espérer, sécher,* etc. – acute accent changes to   3rd person
            grave   plural

       (5) *Envoyer, essuyer, nettoyer* – *y* changes to an i

       (6) *Nous commençons; Nous mangeons*

Irregular -IR Verbs

Some -IR Verbs go like
dormir – to sleep   **courir – to run**

Je dors	Je cours
Tu dors	Tu cours
Il dort	Il court
Elle dort	Elle court
Nous dormons	Nous courons
Vous dormez	Vous courez
Ils dorment	Ils courent
Elles dorment	Elles courent

e.g., partir, to leave; sortir, to go out;
mentir, to (tell a) lie; sentir, to feel;
servir, to serve.

Ouvrir – to open   **Venir – to come**

J'ouvre	Je viens
Tu ouvres	Tu viens
Il ouvre	Il vient
Elle ouvre	Elle vient
Nous ouvrons	Nous venons
Vous ouvrez	Vous venez
Ils ouvrent	Ils viennent
Elles ouvrent	Elles viennent

cf. couvrir, to cover;   cf. tenir, to hold;
    offrir, to offer;   appartenir, to belong;
    souffrir, to suffer.   contenir, to contain;
                                    obtenir, to obtain.

N.B. Endings are those of -ER Verb

Voir – to see

Je vois
Tu vois
Il voit
Elle voit
Nous voyons
Vous voyez
Ils voient
Elles voient

Savoir – to know (a fact)

Je sais
Tu sais
Il sait
Elle sait
Nous savons
Vous savez
Ils savent
Elles savent

Pouvoir – to be able

Je peux
Tu peux
Il peut
Elle peut
Nous pouvons
Vous pouvez
Ils peuvent
Elles peuvent

cf. pleuvoir – to rain (i.e. il pleut)

Vouloir – to wish, to want

Je veux
Tu veux
Il veut
Elle veut
Nous voulons
Vous voulez
Ils veulent
Elles veulent

Valoir – to be worth

Je vaux
Tu vaux
Il vaut
Elle vaut
Nous valons
Vous valez
Ils valent
Elles valent

cf. falloir – to be necessary (i.e. il faut)

S'asseoir - to sit down

Je m'assieds
Tu t'assieds
Il s'assied
Elle s'assied
Nous nous asseyons
Vous vous asseyez
Ils s'asseyent
Elles s'asseyent

Devoir – to owe, to have to, must

Je dois
Tu dois
Il doit
Elle doit
Nous devons
Vous devez
Ils doivent
Elles doivent

Recevoir – to receive

Je reçois
Tu reçois
Il reçoit
Elle reçoit
Nous recevons
Vous recevez
Ils reçoivent
Elles reçoivent

Mourir – to die

Je meurs
Tu meurs
Il meurt
Elle meurt
Nous mourons
Vous mourez
Ils meurent
Elles meurent

Irregular -RE Verbs

Battre – to beat

Je bats
Tu bats   } IRREGULAR
Il bat
Elle bat
Nous battons
Vous battez
Ils battent
Elles battent

cf. mettre, to put;
   admettre, to admit;
   permettre, to allow;
   promettre, to promise.

Prendre – to take

Je prends
Tu prends
Il prend
Elle prend
Nous prenons
Vous prenez   } IRREGULAR
Ils prennent
Elles prennent

cf. comprendre, to understand.

Naître – to be born

Je nais
Tu nais
Il naît
Elle naît
Nous naissons
Vous naissez
Ils naissent
Elles naissent

cf. connaître, to know
(a person or place);
reconnaître, to recognize

Boire – to drink

Je bois
Tu bois
Il boit
Elle boit
Nous buvons
Vous buvez
Ils boivent
Elles boivent

Paraître - to seem, to appear

Je parais
Tu parais
Il paraît
Elle paraît
Nous paraissons
Vous paraissez
Ils paraissent
Elles paraissent

Croire – to think, to believe

Je crois
Tu crois
Il croit
Elle croit
Nous croyons
Vous croyez
Ils croient
Elles croient

Écrire – to write

J'écris
Tu écris
Il écrit
Elle écrit
Nous écrivons
Vous écrivez
Ils écrivent
Elles écrivent

Dire – to say, to tell

Je dis
Tu dis
Il dit
Elle dit
Nous disons
Vous dites
Ils disent
Elles disent

Lire – to read

Je lis
Tu lis
Il lit
Elle lit
Nous lisons
Vous lisez
Ils lisent
Elles lisent

'SAY NO EVIL, READ NO EVIL, NO LAUGHING'...

Rire – to laugh

Je ris
Tu ris
Il rit
Elle rit
Nous rions
Vous riez
Ils rient
Elles rient

Conduire - to lead, to drive

Je conduis
Tu conduis
Il conduit
Elle conduit
Nous conduisons
Vous conduisez
Ils conduisent
Elles conduisent

Suivre – to follow

Je suis
Tu suis
Il suit
Elle suit
Nous suivons
Vous suivez
Ils suivent
Elles suivent

Vivre – to live

Je vis
Tu vis
Il vit
Elle vit
Nous vivons
Vous vivez
Ils vivent
Elles vivent

Craindre – to fear

Je crains
Tu crains
Il craint
Elle craint
Nous craignons
Vous craignez
Ils craignent
Elles craignent

cf. Plaindre, to pity;
    Joindre, to join;
    Peindre, to paint;
    Atteindre, to attain;
    Éteindre, to switch off;

Vaincre – to conquer

Je vaincs
Tu vaincs
Il vainc
Elle vainc
Nous vainquons
Vous vainquez
Ils vainquent
Elles vainquent

cf. Convaincre, to convince

Coudre – to sew

Je couds
Tu couds
Il coud
Elle coud
Nous cousons
Vous cousez
Ils cousent
Elles cousent

'PERFECT TENTS HAVE TWO PARTS'...

1.2   Perfect Tense
(le passé composé or le parfait)

The Perfect Tense always has *two* parts (cf. English – I have given)

Equation

Auxiliary (helper) + past participle = Perfect
i.e. avoir or être

Regular Verbs

-ER → -É   (e.g. donner → j'ai donné)
-IR → -I   (finir → j'ai fini)
-RE → -U   (vendre → j'ai vendu)

Verbs conjugated with Avoir

The vast majority of verbs have *avoir* as their auxiliary.

Irregular Past Participles of Verbs with Avoir

Avoir	(to have)	→	eu
Savoir	(to know)	→	su
Pouvoir	(to be able)	→	pu
Voir	(to see)	→	vu
Pleuvoir	(to rain)	→	plu
Vouloir	(to wish, to want)	→	voulu
Devoir	(to owe; to have to)	→	dû
Recevoir	(to receive)	→	reçu
Courir	(to run)	→	couru
Boire	(to drink)	→	bu
Croire	(to think; to believe)	→	cru
Connaître	(to know)	→	connu
Paraître	(to appear)	→	paru
Lire	(to read)	→	lu

(continued over)

Irregular Past Participles of Verbs with Avoir (cont.)

Rire	(to laugh)	→	ri
Dire	(to say, to tell)	→	dit
Écrire	(to write)	→	écrit
Faire	(to make, to do)	→	fait
Être	(to be)	→	été
Mettre	(to put)	→	mis
Prendre	(to take)	→	pris
Couvrir	(to cover)	→	couvert
Ouvrir	(to open)	→	ouvert
Souffrir	(to suffer)	→	souffert
Offrir	(to offer)	→	offert
Conduire	(to lead)	→	conduit
Vivre	(to live)	→	vécu
Suivre	(to follow)	→	suivi
Tenir	(to hold)	→	tenu
Falloir	(to be necessary)	→	fallu
Apercevoir	(to perceive)	→	aperçu
Coudre	(to sew)	→	cousu
Craindre	(to fear)	→	craint
Joindre	(to join)	→	joint
Peindre	(to paint)	→	peint

Verbs conjugated with être (13)

venir	(to come)	aller	(to go)
entrer	(to come in)	sortir	(to go out)
arriver	(to arrive)	partir	(to depart; leave)
rester	(to stay)	retourner	(to return; go back)
naître	(to be born)	mourir	(to die)
monter	(to go up)	descendre	(to go down)
		tomber	(to fall)

Irregular past participles with être

venir	venu
mourir	mort
naître	né

6 Compounds of the above 13 Verbs

revenir	to come back
devenir	to become
rentrer	to return (home)
ressortir	to go out again
remonter	to go up again
repartir	to set off again

All Reflexive Verbs go with être

e.g.   elle s'est assise – she (has) sat down.

Agreements

With *avoir* the past participle must agree with and only with a preceding direct object (P.D.O.),
e.g.   il les a apportés.
Quelles tables avez-vous vendues?
With *être* the past participle must agree with the subject,
e.g.   Elles sont sorties.

1.3 Pluperfect Tense
(le plus-que-parfait)

Formation of Pluperfect

This is formed by taking the Imperfect of avoir or être instead of the present
and adding the past participle,
e.g.   Nous avions porté   –   We *had* carried.
       Nous étions partis   –   We *had* left.

1.4 Imperfect Tense
(l'imparfait)

Equation

		imperfect endings			
stem of					
1st person plural	+	-ais	-ions		
present tense		-ais	-iez	=	Imperfect
		-ait	-aient		

nous donnons	→	je donnais	–	I was giving
			–	I used to give
nous finissons	→	je finissais	–	I was finishing
			–	I used to finish
nous vendons	→	je vendais	–	I was selling
			–	I used to sell

N.B.   Nous mangeons → je mangeais
          Nous commençons → je commençais

There is only one exception

Être → j'étais – I was; I used to be

1.5 Future Tense
(le futur)

Equation

Infinitive (reg.)	Present Tense		
Future stem (irreg. verbs) +	of avoir (-av)		
-er	-ai	-ons	
-ir	-as	-ez	= Future
-r~~e~~	-a	-ont	

N.B. The future stem always ends in the letter *r*.

e.g. | Je donnerai | – | I shall (will) give |
|---|---|---|
| Je finirai | – | I shall finish |
| Je vendrai | – | I shall sell |

Irregular Verbs

aller	(to go)	→	j'irai
venir	(to come)	→	je viendrai
tenir	(to hold)	→	je tiendrai
être	(to be)	→	je serai
faire	(to do; to make)	→	je ferai
avoir	(to have)	→	j'aurai
savoir	(to know)	→	je saurai
courir	(to run)	→	je courrai
mourir	(to die)	→	je mourrai
pouvoir	(to be able)	→	je pourrai
vouloir	(to wish, to want)	→	je voudrai
devoir	(to owe, to have to)	→	je devrai
recevoir	(to receive)	→	je recevrai
pleuvoir	(to rain)	→	il pleuvra
voir	(to see)	→	je verrai
envoyer	(to send)	→	j'enverrai
s'asseoir	(to sit down)	→	je m'assiérai
falloir	(to be necessary)	→	il faudra

Logical Future

Remember that French requires the future when futurity is implied,
e.g. I will see you when you *come back,*
　　Je te verrai quand tu *reviendras.*

Use after the following conjunctions:

Quand   }
Lorsque }　=　　**When**　　　Aussitôt }
　　　　　　　　　　　　Dès que }　=　　As soon as

1.6　Conditional Tense
(le conditionnel)

Equation

Infinitive (reg. verbs)		imperfect			
Future stem (irreg. verbs)	+	endings		=	Conditional
donner		-ais	-ions		
finir		-ais	-iez		
vendre		-ait	-aient		

e.g.　　tomber　　→　　je tomberais　　–　　I would fall
　　　　aller　　　→　　j'irais　　　　 　–　　I would go

DONNEZ!

BUTIN

THE IMPERATIVE...

1.7 Imperative Mood

The forms of the imperative are the 2nd person singular and plural, and the 1st person plural of the present tense, with the subject removed.

Donner

donne! – give!
donnons! – let us give!
donnez! – give!

Finir

finis! – finish!
finissons! – let us finish!
finissez! – finish!

Vendre

vends! – sell!
vendons! – let us sell!
vendez! – sell!

N.B. The 's' is dropped from the 2nd person singular if the last vowel is an 'e'.
This also applies to aller:

va! – go!
allons! – let us go!
allez! – go!

There are only 3 exceptions

Être

sois! – be!
soyons! – let us be!
soyez! – be!

Avoir

aie! – have!
ayons! – let us have!
ayez! – have!

Savoir

sache! know!
sachons! let us know!
sachez! know!

Remember that in the case of the imperative affirmative (positive command) the object pronouns must follow the verb,

e.g.   Regardez-moi!   –   look at me!   Assieds-toi! ⎫
       Donnez-le-moi!   –   give it to me!   Asseyez-vous! ⎬ – sit down!

1.8 Infinitives

Where there are two verbs, the second is always put into the infinitive (cf. position of the object pronouns).

1.9 Present Participles

These are formed by adding *-ant* (*-ing* in English) to the stem of the nrst person plural present tense (i.e. the 'nous' form),

e.g.   nous finissons → finissant − finishing

There are only 3 exceptions:

être	→	étant	− being
avoir	→	ayant	− having
savoir	→	sachant	− knowing

Uses

(1)   As an adjective (with agreement),
        e.g. des histoires amusant*es* – amusing stories.
(2)   With verbal force (no agreement),
        e.g. ayant faim il a vite mangé – being hungry he ate quickly.
(3)   With *en* meaning while, by, in, on (doing something),
        e.g. en se promenant dans la forêt – while walking in the forest.

BUT do not over-use present participle. Its uses are much more restricted than in English, i.e. I am giving = Je donne.

1.10   Verbs followed by à

Verbs followed by à + infinitive

apprendre à	–	to learn to
commencer à } se mettre à }	–	to begin to
continuer à	–	to continue to
réussir à	–	to manage to, to succeed in
se décider à	–	to decide to
se préparer à	–	to prepare to

Verbs followed by à + noun

commander à	–	to order
conseiller à	–	to advise
défendre à	–	to forbid
demander à	–	to ask
désobéir à	–	to disobey
dire à	–	to tell
obéir à	–	to obey
ordonner à	–	to order
pardonner à	–	to forgive
permettre à	–	to allow, to permit
plaire à	–	to please
promettre à	–	to promise
rendre visite à	–	to visit (someone)
répondre à	–	to answer
résister à	–	to resist
ressembler à	–	to look like
servir à	–	to serve
téléphoner à	–	to ring, to phone

Note the following construction:
commander, conseiller, défendre, demander, dire, ordonner, permettre, promettre . . . à quelqu'un de faire quelque chose,

e.g.   Je dis à Jean de se lever – I tell John to get up.
Sa mère lui permet de sortir – His mother lets him go out.

N.B.   Répondez à la question → Répondez-y – answer it.
Obéissez aux instructions → Obéissez-y – obey them.

1.11   Verbs followed by de

Verbs followed by de + infinitive

cesser de	–	to cease to
continuer de	–	to continue to
décider de	–	to decide to
essayer de	–	to try to
finir de	–	to stop
offrir de	–	to offer to
oublier de	–	to forget to
refuser de	–	to refuse to
regretter de	–	to regret
s'arrêter de	–	to stop

Verbs followed by de + noun

partir de	–	to leave
s'approcher de	–	to approach
se douter de	–	to suspect
s'occuper de	–	to take care of
se servir de	–	to use
se souvenir de	–	to remember
se tromper de	–	to make a mistake

Note the following examples:

Servez-vous-en	–	use it
Elle s'en occupe	–	she is looking after it
Je m'en souviendrai	–	I shall remember it
Je me suis trompé de cahier	–	I have brought the wrong exercise book
Elle s'est trompée de route	–	she took the wrong route

'Jouer de' and 'jouer à'

Jouer de is used with musical instruments,
    e.g. Je joue du trombone, du violon et de la guitare.
Jouer à is used with games and sports,
    e.g. Je joue au tennis et aux échecs.

'Penser de' and 'penser à'

Penser de means 'to think' in the sense of 'to have an opinion',
e.g. Que pensez-vous de lui? – What do you think of him?
Penser à means 'to think' as a mental process,
e.g. À quoi pensez-vous? – what are you thinking about?

1.12 entrer dans

N.B. Le garçon est entré dans la salle de classe –

the boy entered the classroom

1.13 Some French Verbs which include the English Preposition

attendre	–	to wait for
chercher	–	to look for
demander	–	to ask for
écouter	–	to listen to
envoyer chercher	–	to send for
habiter	–	to live in
payer	–	to pay for
regarder	–	to look at
soigner	–	to care for
viser	–	to aim at

1.14 The Passive Voice

Formation: *être* in any of its tenses + past participle of a transitive verb.
(A transitive verb is one which can take a direct object)

e.g.	Present	–	je suis vu(e)	–	I am seen
	Perfect	–	j'ai été vu(e)	–	I have been seen
	Imperfect	–	j'étais vu(e)	–	I was seen
	Future	–	je serai vu(e)	–	I will be seen

N.B. As *être* is used, the past participle must agree with the subject.

(continued over)

(Passive Voice continued)

'By' after a verb in the passive is usually translated by *par*.
e.g.   Il sera puni par le proviseur – he will be punished by the Head Master.

But note: Il était accompagné *de* ses enfants –
                              he was accompanied by his children.
Elle est aimée *de* tout le monde – she is liked by everyone.

Avoidance of the Passive

The passive voice is used less frequently in French than it is in English and
there are two common ways of avoiding it.

(1)   By making the sentence active with 'on' as the subject,

e.g. on l'a arrêté – he was arrested;
     ici on parle anglais – English (is) spoken here;
     on lui a fait payer une amende – he was forced to pay a fine.

N.B. The indirect object cannot be turned round to become the subject of
the French passive construction, as we often do in English,

e.g. On m'a donné un cadeau – I was given a present.
     On lui a dit la vérité – He was told the truth.

(2)   By using a reflexive verb,
      e.g. Je m'appelle Jacques – I am called James.
      Comment cela se dit-il en français? – How is that said in French?
      Comment s'est-il habillé? – How was he dressed?

2 NOUNS

2.1 Gender of Nouns

Words ending in	Usually	Common Exceptions
-age	Masculine	la page; la plage; la rage; la cage; la nage; une image
-aire	Masculine	
-al	Masculine	
-ance	Feminine	
-cycle	Masculine	
-eau	Masculine	l'eau; la peau
-ème	Masculine	
-ence	Feminine	le silence
-ent	Masculine	la dent
-er	Masculine	la mer
-et	Masculine	la forêt
-ette	Feminine	le squelette
-eu	Masculine	
-eur	Masculine (if person)	
-eur	Feminine (if not)	le bonheur; le malheur; l'honneur; le moteur; le radiateur
-euse	Feminine	
-isme	Masculine	
-ment	Masculine	la jument
-(m)ure	Feminine	
-ou	Masculine	
-tion	Feminine	

Nouns with 2 Genders

le livre (book);	la livre (pound)
le manche (handle);	la manche (sleeve);
	la Manche (English Channel)
le page (page boy);	la page (page)
le poêle (stove);	la poêle (frying pan)
le poste (post, position)	la poste (post, post office)
le somme (nap);	la somme (sum of money)
le tour (trick, turn, tour);	la tour (tower)
le vague (vagueness);	la vague (wave)
le vase (vase);	la vase (river mud)

2.2   Plurals of Nouns

To make a noun plural we usually add 's', but there are some exceptions.

Words Ending in	Plural	Examples
-al	-aux	les animaux; les journaux; les chev*aux*
-eau	-x	les bateaux; les cadeaux; les châteaux
-eu	-x	les jeux; les feux; les chev*eux*
-s	No change	les bras; les bois
-x	No change	les voix
-z	No change	les nez

Words in *-ou* take a plural in 's', e.g. les trous.
But 7 only take a plural in 'x':

Viz.	le chou	–	cabbage	le hibou	–	owl
	le genou	–	knee	le joujou	–	toy
	le bijou	–	jewel	le pou	–	louse
	le caillou	–	pebble			

Note also

Un oeil bleu	→	des *yeux* bleu*s*
le travail	→	les trav*aux*
la grand' mère	→	les grand' mères
le ciel	→	les cieux
monsieur; madame	→	messieurs; mesdames

ORDER OF PRONOUNS (FOOTBALL TEAM FORMATION)

3 PRONOUNS

3.1 Personal Pronouns

Subject		Conjunctive (Weak) Direct Obj.	Indirect Obj.		Reflexive Obj.		(Strong) Disjunctive
1 Je	*I*	Me	*Me*	Me	*To Me*	Me	*Myself*	Moi
2 Tu	*You*	Te	*You*	Te	*To You*	Te	*Yourself*	Toi
3 Il	*He*	Le	*Him*	Lui	*To Him* *To Her*	Se	*Himself* *Herself*	Lui
Elle	*She*	La	*Her*					Elle
1 Nous	*We*	Nous	*Us*	Nous	*To Us*	Nous	*Ourselves*	Nous
2 Vous	*You*	Vous	*You*	Vous	*To You*	Vous	*Yourselves*	Vous
3 Ils Elles	*They*	Les	*Them*	Leur	*To Them*	Se	*Themselves*	Eux Elles
On	*One*					Se	*Oneself*	Soi

N.B. Y = there
A preposition + Noun is often replaced by *Y.*
e.g. Il entre dans la maison → Il *y* entre.

En = some, any, of it, of them, from it, from them.
De + Noun replaced by *En,*
e.g. J'ai besoin de votre aide → J'*en* ai besoin.
No agreement with *En!*

Order of Object Pronouns

me					
te	le	lui			
se	la	leur	y	en	Verb
nous	les				
vous		(Football team formation)			

When there is more than one object pronoun in a sentence the above order is followed.

Position of Object Pronouns in a sentence

The object pronoun comes *before the verb.*

(a)   When there is *one* verb in a sentence in the Perfect tense the object
        pronoun comes *immediately before the auxiliary verb,*
        e.g. il l'a porté.

(b)   When there are *two* verbs in a sentence the second is in the infinitive,
        and the object pronoun comes *immediately before the infinitive,*
        e.g. nous allons le trouver.

N.B.   There is *one* case where the object pronoun *follows the verb,* i.e. a
        positive command. This is the case where you are telling someone to
        do something,
        e.g. Regardez-moi!; ouvrez-les!

In this case *me* and *te* become *moi* and *toi,* and one puts a hyphen between the
verb and pronoun.
The order is thus:

		-moi		
		-toi		
	-le	-nous		
Verb	-la	-vous	-y	-en
	-les	-lui		
		-leur		(English word order)

But *me* and *te* do not change before y or *en,*
e.g.   assieds-t'y – sit there; prêtez-m'en – lend me some.

Use of Disjunctive Pronouns

(1)   *After* a preposition, e.g. avec eux – with them.

(2)   *After* C'est and Ce sont; e.g. c'est moi – it is I.

(3)   *After* que in a comparison;
        e.g. Je suis plus grand que toi – I am taller than you.

(4)   *For emphasis;* e.g. vous, vous êtes stupide.

(5)   *Replacing noun standing on its own;*
        e.g. Qui a dit cela? Lui? Non, elle.

3.2 Interrogative Pronouns

These replace interrogative adjective *quel* etc. + noun.

	Masculine		*Feminine*	
Singular	lequel?	Which one?	laquelle?	Which one?
Plural	lesquels?	Which ones?	lesquelles?	Which ones?

3.3 Demonstrative Pronouns

These replace demonstrative adjective *ce, cette, ces* + noun.

	Masculine		*Feminine*	
Singular	Celui	This one, the one	Celle	This one, the one
Plural	Ceux	These, those	Celles	These, those

They must be followed by either:
    (a) qui; que; dont;
or (b) de;
or (c) -ci; -là.

N.B. 'The former' – celui-là; celle-là, etc.
        'The latter' – celui-ci; celle-ci, etc.

3.4 Relative Pronouns

Subject	*qui*	–	who, which
Direct Object	*que(qu')*	–	whom, which
Possessive	*dont*	–	whose, of whom
After Preposition	*lequel, laquelle, lesquels, lesquelles* – which		

e.g.   C'est un garçon *qui* a beaucoup d'amis.
        Le garçon, *que* je connais, a beaucoup d'amis.
        Le livre, *dont* vous avez besoin, est sur la table.
        Le stylo, *avec lequel* il écrit, coûte cher.

N.B. à + lequel → auquel;   de + lequel → duquel
        à + lesquels → auxquels; de + lesquels → desquels

How to distinguish between *QUI* and *QUE*

Qui (subject) and que (object) can both mean *which.*
BUT remember this golden rule, and you will avoid errors.

qui   *+ Verb.*
que   *+ Noun or Pronoun*
e.g.   La robe de fête, *que* sa mère a achetée, et *qu'* elle aime le mieux,
       est celle *qui* a été déchirée.

THE KEY WORD!

3.5   Possessive Pronouns

These replace possessive adjective *mon, ma, mes etc.* + noun.

	Singular		Plural	
Masculine	*Feminine*	*Masculine*	*Feminine*
le mien	*mine*	la mienne	les miens	les miennes
le tien	*yours*	la tienne	les tiens	les tiennes
le sien	*his, hers*	la sienne	les siens	les siennes
le nôtre	*ours*	la nôtre	les nôtres	les nôtres
le vôtre	*yours*	la vôtre	les vôtres	les vôtres
le leur	*theirs*	la leur	les leurs	les leurs

4   ADJECTIVES

4.1   Agreement of adjective with noun

In the normal way adjectives form their feminine by adding *-e*, their masculine plural by adding *-s*, and their feminine plural by adding *-es*. Thus:

	Singular	Plural
Masculine	-	-s
Feminine	-e	-es

But those adjectives ending in a silent *-e* do not add another *-e* in the feminine – they remain the same,

e.g.   Un livre rouge; une voiture rouge.

RULE: Never write two silent *e*'s together. The first must always have an accent, e.g. la poupée, il l' a créée.

Irregular Agreements

Masculine			Feminine	
premier	[er]	*first*	première	[ère]
curieux	[x]	*curious*	curieuse	[se]
actif	[f]	*active*	active	[ve]
criminel	[el]	*criminal*	criminelle	[elle]
parisien	[en]	*parisian*	parisienne	[enne]
muet	[et]	*dumb*	muette	[ette]
bon	[on]	*good*	bonne	[onne]
gras	[as]	*fat*	grasse	[asse]
pareil	[eil]	*similar*	pareille	[eille]
blanc		*white*	blanche	
long		*long*	longue	
doux		*sweet*	douce	
faux		*false*	fausse	
gros		*big*	grosse	
épais		*thick*	épaisse	
sot		*foolish*	sotte	
gentil		*kind*	gentille	
sec		*dry*	sèche	
favori		*favourite*	favorite	
frais		*fresh*	fraîche	
public		*public*	publique	

Irregular agreements (cont.)

BUT

Masculine			Feminine
secret	*secret*	→	secrète
complet	*complete*	→	complète
discret	*discreet*	→	discrète
inquiet	*anxious*	→	inquiète

Some adjectives have a distinct form in the masculine singular before a noun beginning with a vowel or silent *h*.

Singular

Masculine		Masculine before vowel	Feminine
beau	*beautiful*	bel	belle
nouveau	*new*	nouvel	nouvelle
vieux	*old*	vieil	vieille
fou	*mad*	fol	folle
mou	*soft*	mol	molle

Plural

Masculine			Feminine	
beau bel	→	beaux; belle	→	belles
vieux vieil	→	vieux; vieille	→	vieilles

Remember that an old woman has two *eyes,*
e.g.   La vie*i*lle – the old woman,
        La ve*i*lle – the eve, preceding day.

4.2 Position of Adjectives in relation to noun

The *vast majority* of adjectives *follow the noun:*

e.g. Un mur *bas*   –   a *low* wall
Une porte *verte*   –   a *green* door
Des histoires *amusantes*   –   *amusing* stories

The following adjectives usually *precede the noun:*

bon	*good*	beau	*beautiful*
mauvais	*bad*	joli	*pretty*
petit	*small*	vilain	*mean; ugly*
grand	*big; great*	méchant	*naughty; wicked*
gros	*big; stout*	gentil	*kind*
vieux	*old*	haut	*high*
jeune	*young*	vaste	*vast*
nouveau	*new*	meilleur	*better*
long	*long*	ancien	*former, ex.*
premier	*first*	dernier	*final*

4.3 Interrogative Adjectives

	Masculine		*Feminine*	
Singular	Quel?	Which? What?	Quelle?	Which? etc.
Plural	Quels?	Which?	Quelles?	Which?

4.4 Demonstrative Adjectives

	Masculine		*Masc. before vowel*		*Feminine*	
Singular	Ce	this, that	Cet	this, that	Cette	this, that
Plural	←		Ces	these, those	→	

4.5 Possessive Adjectives

Masculine		*Feminine*	*Plural*
mon	*my*	ma	mes
ton	*your*	ta	tes
son	*his, her*	sa	ses
notre	*our*	notre	nos
votre	*your*	votre	vos
leur	*their*	leur	leurs

5 ADVERBS

5.1 Formation

To form the adverb from the adjective add -*ment* (= *ly* in English) if the adjective ends in a vowel,
e.g.   stupide → stupidement – *stupidly.*

If the adjective ends in a consonant then make it feminine first,
e.g.   dernier → dernièrement – *lastly.*

If the adjective ends in -*nt* then change to -*m* before you add -*ment*,
e.g.   courant → couramment – *fluently,*
        violent → violemment – *violently.*

5.2 Common Irregular Adverbs

lent	→	lentement	–	*slowly*
vite	→	vite	–	*quickly, fast*
bon	→	bien	–	*well*
mauvais	→	mal	–	*badly*
petit	→	peu	–	*little*
meilleur	→	mieux	–	*better*
gai	→	gaiement	–	*gaily*
fou	→	follement	–	*madly*
mou	→	mollement	–	*softly*
gentil	→	gentiment	–	*kindly*
énorme	→	énormément	–	*enormously*
précis	→	précisément	–	*precisely*
profond	→	profondément	–	*deeply*

6 PREPOSITIONS

6.1 Some Important Prepositions

(1)	sur	–	on	(4)	devant	–	in front of
(2)	sous	–	under	(5)	avec	–	with
(3)	derrière	–	behind	(6)	sans	–	without

(7)	avant	– before	(17)	vers	– towards
(8)	après	– after	(18)	contre	– against
(9)	dans	– in; into	(19)	près de	– near to
(10)	à	– to; at; in	(20)	loin de	– far from
(11)	en	– in; to	(21)	par	– through; by
(12)	de	– of; from	(22)	à travers	– through; across
(13)	entre	– between	(23)	chez	– at (to) the house of
(14)	pour	– for; in order to	(24)	parmi	– among
(15)	pendant	– during; for	(25)	malgré	– in spite of; despite
(16)	depuis	– since; for			

N.B.   *To at* or *in* a town = *à,*
e.g. à Paris; à Londres; à Edimbourg; à Douvres; au Havre.
To or *in* a country = *en,*
e.g. en France; en Angleterre.
BUT with masculine countries (those not ending in a silent -*e*)
use *au; aux,*
In a county = *dans le,* e.g. dans le Devon.
Note the exception *en* Cornouailles = in Cornwall.

6.2   Countries

Some Masculine Countries

au	Canada	–	in Canada
au	Portugal	–	in Portugal
au	Danemark	–	in Denmark
au	Japon	–	in Japan
au	Pays de Galles	–	in Wales
aux	États Unis	–	in the United States
aux	Antilles	–	in the West Indies
aux	Pays-Bas	–	in the Netherlands

Some Feminine Countries

en	France	–	in France
en	Angleterre	–	in England
en	Écosse	–	in Scotland
en	Irlande	–	in Ireland

(continued over)

Some Feminine Countries (cont.)

en	Italie	–	in Italy
en	Espagne	–	in Spain
en	Belgique	–	in Belgium
en	Hollande	–	in Holland
en	Suisse	–	in Switzerland
en	Allemagne	–	in Germany
en	Autriche	–	in Austria
en	Norvège	–	in Norway
en	Suède	–	in Sweden
en	Finlande	–	in Finland
en	Russie	–	in Russia
en	Grèce	–	in Greece
en	Inde	–	in India
en	Chine	–	in China

6.3   The Continents

en	Europe	–	in Europe
en	Asie	–	in Asia
en	Amérique	–	in America
en	Afrique	–	in Africa
en	Australie	–	in Australia

6.4   Prepositional Phrases

There is considerable subtlety in the way prepositions are used in French, and the literal translation must often be avoided. The following prepositional phrases should prove both useful and enlightening.

au soleil	–	in the sun
sous la pluie	–	in the rain
à l'ombre	–	in the shade
par un temps pareil	–	in such weather
de cette manière	–	in this way
à la campagne	–	in the countryside
en ville	–	in town
de nos jours	–	in our time, nowadays
sous le règne de	–	in the reign of
la dame aux lunettes	–	the lady in the glasses
le plus petit garçon de la classe	–	the smallest boy in the class
pendant les vacances	–	in the holidays

dans une ferme	–	on a farm
au tableau noir	–	on the blackboard
la carte pend au mur	–	the map is hanging on the wall
par terre	–	on the ground
par une journée d'été	–	on a summer's day
par politesse	–	out of politeness
huit sur dix	–	eight out of ten
en bois	–	made (out) of wood
en brique	–	made (out) of brick
en pierre	–	made (out) of stone
en verre	–	made (out) of glass
un sac en plastique	–	a plastic bag
deux fois par an	–	twice a year
à pied	–	on foot
à vélo; à bicyclette	–	by bike
en auto; en voiture	–	by car
en train	–	by train
en bateau	–	by boat
en avion	–	by plane
vers une heure	–	about one o'clock
aux yeux bruns	–	with brown eyes
il est fâché contre moi	–	he is angry with me
il a bu dans le verre	–	he drank from the glass
il l'a pris dans le tiroir	–	he took it out of the drawer
il l'a pris sur le rayon	–	he took it off the shelf
il a changé d'avis	–	he changed his mind
il me parle en ami	–	he speaks to me as a friend

7 NEGATIVES

ne...	pas	–	not
ne...	pas du tout	–	not at all
ne...	plus	–	no more; no longer
ne...	rien	–	nothing
ne...	jamais	–	never
ne...	que	–	only; nothing but; except for
ne...	personne	–	no-one; nobody
ne...	ni... ni	–	neither... nor
ne...	guère	–	scarcely; hardly

(continued over)

Negatives (cont.)

ne...	aucun			
ne...	nul(le)	–	no, none	(literary)
ne...	nulle part	–	nowhere	
ne...	point	–	not (at all)	(literary)

N.B. Je n'ai rien dit – I have said nothing,

but Je n'ai vu *personne* – I have seen no-one.

i.e. *Personne* and *nulle part* must follow the past participle.

Rien and *personne* can also be the subject of a sentence.

e.g. *Rien n'*est perdu – nothing is lost.

*Personne n'*est arrivé – nobody has arrived.

In this case *rien* and *personne* are not complete without *ne* before the verb.

8 USES OF DE

The partitive article (*du, de la, de l', des*) is shortened to *de* or *d':*

(1)   *After* a negative,

e.g. Je n'ai pas *de* pommes.

(2)   *After* an expression of quantity,

e.g. Il a beaucoup *de* livres.

beaucoup	–	much; many; a lot;	**combien**	–	how much; how many
trop	–	too much; too many;	**assez**	–	enough
tant	–	so much; so many;	**peu**	–	little

(3)   *Before* an adjective + noun in the plural,

e.g. Il porte *de* grands cahiers.

But Il porte *des* cahiers rouges,

because it is a noun + adjective in the plural.

9 IDIOMS
9.1 Idioms with '*avoir*'

avoir froid	–	to be cold
avoir chaud	–	to be hot
avoir faim	–	to be hungry
avoir soif	–	to be thirsty

avoir raison	–	to be right
avoir tort	–	to be wrong
avoir peur	–	to be afraid
avoir sommeil	–	to be sleepy
avoir honte	–	to be ashamed
avoir lieu	–	to take place
avoir l'air	–	to seem
avoir besoin de	–	to need
avoir envie de	–	to want
avoir mal à	–	to have something wrong with

N.B. Nous *avons* chaud – We are hot
Il *fait* chaud – It is hot weather
L'eau *est* chaude – The water is hot

9.2   Idioms with *faire*

Il fait beau (temps)	–	It is fine weather
Il fait mauvais (temps)	–	It is bad weather
Il fait chaud	–	It is hot
Il fait froid	–	It is cold
Il fait frais	–	It is cool
Il fait jour	–	It is daylight
Il fait nuit	–	It is dark
Il fait sombre	–	It is dark
Il fait du soleil	–	It is sunny
Il fait du vent	–	It is windy
Il fait du brouillard	–	It is foggy
Il fait de l'orage	–	It is thundering
Il fait un temps couvert	–	It is overcast; cloudy
Il fait un temps affreux	–	The weather is awful
Il fait un temps superbe	–	The weather is splendid

9.3   *Venir de* + infinitive

Venir de + infinitive = to have just done something.
It is used in the *present* or the *imperfect*,
e.g.   Ils *viennent de* sortir – They *have* just gone out.
    Ils *venaient de* sortir – They *had* just gone out.
In English we use the *perfect* or the *pluperfect* respectively.

9.4   Tenses with *depuis*

Similarly *depuis* (since) used with the *present* or the *imperfect* translates an
action or state in the past, which is still going on at the present time:
e.g.   Ils *sont* ici *depuis* une semaine.
      They *have been* here *for* a week.   (English *perfect*)
e.g.   Ils *étaient* ici *depuis* une semaine.
      They *had been* here *for* a week.   (English *pluperfect*)

9.5   Être en train de

Être en train de – to be occupied in.
e.g.   Je suis *en train de* faire mes devoirs.
      I am *engaged in* doing my homework.

9.6   C'est; Il est

Use *c'est* with a noun or pronoun,
e.g.   *c'est un homme.; c'est lui.*

N.B.   Il est professeur.   (Omit the indefinite article)
       C'est *un* professeur.

ACCENT ON A GRAVE SITUATION

PART B
MISCELLANEOUS INFORMATION

10.1 Distinguish between . . .

(1)	écouter	–	to listen to
(2)	entendre	–	to hear
(3)	attendre	–	to wait for
(4)	assister à	–	to attend
(5)	aider	–	to assist
(1)	montrer	–	to show; to point to
(2)	monter	–	to climb up
(3)	mentir	–	to (tell a) lie
(1)	retourner	–	to return (go back)
(2)	revenir	–	to return (come back)
(3)	rentrer	–	to return (home)
(4)	rendre	–	to return (give back)

10.2 Les Accents

(é)	–	accent aigu (acute), e.g. l'été
(è)	–	accent grave (grave), e.g. le père
(ê)	–	accent circonflexe (circumflex), e.g. être
(ç)	–	accent cédille (cedilla), e.g. le garçon
(ë)	–	tréma (diaeresis), e.g. Noël

N.B. Circumflex usually indicates an *s* has been omitted
(*château* – castle).
Cedilla softens a hard *c* (nous commençons).
Tréma indicates that two vowels should be pronounced
independently of one another (contrast diphthong
la soeur).

10.3 L'Alphabet Français

To know the French alphabet is essential! The following guide may help you to learn and remember it:

(✓) F, L, M, N, O, S, Z   are similar to their English counterparts.
(x) B, C, D,G, P, T, V, W,   rhyme with the English word *bay*.
      I, J   rhyme with each other.
      K, R   sound like *car* and *air*.

Thus:

A	E	I ⎫ rhyme	M ✓	Q	U	Y (i grec)
B x	F ✓	J ⎭	N ✓	R (air)	V x	Z ✓
C x	G x	K (car)	O ✓	S ✓	W x	
D x	H	L ✓	P x	T x	X	

10.4 Days – Les Jours de la Semaine

lundi	–	Monday
mardi	–	Tuesday
mercredi	–	Wednesday
jeudi	–	Thursday
vendredi	–	Friday
samedi	–	Saturday
dimanche	–	Sunday

DAYS OF THE WEEK

(Moon, Mars, Mercury, Jupiter, Venus, Saturn, Lord's Day)

10.5   Months – Les Mois de l'Année

janvier	–	January
février	–	February
mars	–	March
avril	–	April
mai	–	May
juin	–	June
juillet	–	July
août	–	August
septembre	–	September
octobre	–	October
novembre	–	November
décembre	–	December

10.6   Seasons – Les Quatre Saisons de l'Année

Le printemps	–	Spring	*au* printemps	–	*in* Spring
l'été (m)	–	Summer	*en* été	–	*in* Summer
l'automne (m. or f.)	–	Autumn	*en* automne	–	*in* Autumn
l'hiver (m.)	–	Winter	*en* hiver	–	*in* Winter

10.7   Numbers – Les Nombres Cardinaux

1.	un; une	13.	treize	50.	cinquante
2.	deux	14.	quatorze	60.	soixante
3.	trois	15.	quinze	70.	soixante-dix
4.	quatre	16.	seize	71.	soixante *et* onze
5.	cinq	17.	dix-sept	80.	quatre-vingts
6.	six	18.	dix-huit	81.	quatre-vingt-un
7.	sept	19.	dix-neuf	90.	quatre-vingt-dix
8.	huit	20.	vingt	100.	cent
9.	neuf	21.	vingt *et* un	200.	deux cents
10.	dix	22.	vingt-deux	201.	deux cent un
11.	onze	30.	trente	1000.	mille
12.	douze	40.	quarante	2000.	deux mille

Note also:

dizaine	–	(about) 10;	vingtaine	–	(about) 20; a score
douzaine	–	(about) 12; dozen	quarantaine	–	(about) 40; quarantine
quinzaine	–	(about) 15; fortnight	centaine	–	(about) 100

Les Nombres Ordinaux

1st	–	premier	5th	–	cinquième
2nd	–	deuxième; second	9th	–	neuvième
3rd	–	troisième	21st	–	vingt et *unième*
4th	–	quatrième	1000th	–	millième

10.8   Date – La Date

But dates are written with cardinal numbers
e.g. vendredi, le vingt-six mars.

Except for the first of the month
e.g. jeudi, le premier août.
DATES MUST BE WRITTEN IN small letters.

10.9   Time (l'heure)

Note the following examples:

Il est une heure cinq	– It is five past one
Il est deux heures dix	– It is ten past two
Il est trois heures et quart	– It is quarter past three
Il est quatre heures vingt-cinq	– It is twenty five past four
Il est cinq heures et demie	– It is half past five
Il est six heures moins vingt	– It is twenty to six
Il est sept heures moins le quart	– It is quarter to seven
Il est huit heures du matin	– It is eight o'clock in the morning
Il est deux heures de l'après-midi	– It is two o'clock in the afternoon
Il est neuf heures du soir	– It is nine o'clock in the evening
Il est midi	– It is midday
Il est midi et quart	– It is quarter past twelve (noon)
Il est midi vingt	– It is twenty past twelve (12.20 p.m.)
Il est midi et demi	– It is half past twelve (12.30 p.m.)
Il est minuit moins le quart	– It is quarter to twelve (11.45 p.m.)
Il est minuit moins cinq	– It is five to twelve (11.55 p.m.)
Il est minuit	– It is midnight
Il est minuit et demi	– It is half past twelve (12.30 a.m.)

PART C

11 COMPREHENSION

11.1 Question Words

(1)	Pourquoi?	–	Why? (Answer usually requires *parce que*)
(2)	Où?	–	Where?
(3)	Quand?	–	When?
(4)	Comment?	–	How? What? What . . . like?
(5)	Combien?	–	How much? How many?
(6)	Qui?	–	Who?
(7)	Que?	–	What?
(8)	Qu'est-ce que?	–	What?
(9)	Est-ce que?	–	Is it that?
(10)	Quel + noun?	–	Which? What?
(11)	De quelle couleur?	–	What colour?
(12)	Depuis quand?	–	How long?
(13)	À quoi sert?	–	To what use? For what purpose?

11.2 Important Questions

1. Q. Comment vous appelez-vous?
   A. Je m'appelle Michel Blanc.

2. Q. Quel âge avez-vous?
   A. J'ai treize ans.

3. Q. Où habitez-vous?
   A. J'habite (à) Paris.

4. Q. Comment allez-vous?
   A. Je vais très bien, merci.

5. Q. Quelle heure est-il?
   A. Il est deux heures et demie.

6. Q. Quel temps fait-il?
   A. Il fait beau.

7. Q. Quel jour sommes-nous aujourd'hui?
   A. Aujourd'hui nous sommes lundi.

8. Q. Quelle est la date aujourd'hui?
   A. La date est mardi, le quatorze juillet.

9. Q. Combien d'élèves y a-t-il dans votre classe?
   A. Il y en a vingt-cinq.

PART D

12 PRONUNCIATION

12.1 Sounds

Here are some rules which should help your spelling.

The following letters or combinations of letters are *all* pronounced rather like *A*, the first letter of the English alphabet:

1)	*-er*	cf.	donn*er*
2)	*-ez*	cf.	vous donn*ez*
3)	*-é*	cf.	j'ai donn*é*
4)	*-ai*	cf.	j'*ai*; je donner*ai*
5)	*-et*	cf.	*et* (= and)

The following letters or combinations of letters are pronounced [*e*] as in the English word 'red':

1)	*es*	cf.	tu *es*
2)	*est*	cf.	il *est*
3)	*-ais*	cf.	je donn*ais* (imperfect tense)
4)	*-ait*	cf.	il finir*ait* (conditional tense)
5)	*-aient*	cf.	ils vend*aient*
6)	*ê*	cf.	*ê*tre; la fen*ê*tre
7)	*è*	cf.	le p*è*re (long vowel sound)

N.B. Distinguish carefully between *et* (and): *est* (is).

[i] The French letter *i* is pronounced like the English letter *e*.
e.g. il d*i*t.

[ou] The letters *ou* are pronounced like the English word 'boo'.
e.g. un s*ou*; le b*ou*t.

[au] The letters *au* and *eau* are pronounced like the English word *oh*!
[eau] e.g. *au*; ch*au*d.
l'*eau*; b*eau*; le chap*eau*.

[eu] The letters *eu* are pronounced as in French word 'n*eu*f'.
Exception: J'ai *eu* (*u* sound).

[eur] The letters *eur* are pronounced like the English word *sir* but with a guttural *r*,
e.g. l*eur*; l'h*eur*e.

[oi]   The letters *oi* are pronounced as in the English word *won*,
       e.g. un *oi*seau; le b*oi*s.
[u]   This represents a combination of *oo* and *ee*,
       e.g. d*u;* le b*u*t; s*u*r.
       One forms the lips to say *oo* and tries to say the *ee* sound.

Contrast the difference between:

(1) au-dess*us*   –   above   (1) le b*u*t   –   goal; aim
(2) au-dess*ous* –   below   (2) le b*ou*t –   end

[h]   NEVER PRONOUNCE the *h*, e.g. un *h*omme.
[th]   pronounced as *t*, e.g. le *th*éâtre.
[s]   pronounced *z* (in middle of word), e.g. le va*s*e; la mai*s*on.
       pronounced *s* (at beginning), e.g. *s*ortir.
[ss]   pronounced *s* (in middle of word), e.g. re*ss*ortir.
[l]   pronounced *l*, e.g. un é*l*ève.
       but note *le fils* (rhymes with English *peace*).
[ll]   Sometimes – *ll*, e.g. la vi*ll*e; le vi*ll*age; be*ll*e.
       Sometimes silent, e.g. la fi*ll*e (cf. English f*ee*).
[c;g] are hard when followed by *A, O, U*, e.g. la *g*are; comme,
       but soft when followed by *E, I*, e.g. i*c*i; â*g*e.
       To make a hard *c* or *g* soft we use the following:
       (1) ç, e.g. le gar*ç*on; nous commen*ç*ons,
       (2) *e* after the *g*, e.g. nous man*ge*ons.

12.2 Homonyms

The following words often cause problems because they have the same (or
almost the same) pronunciation.

1) il   – he   2) elle   – she
   ils   – they   elles – they
3) la   – the   4) son   – his, her
   là   – there   sont   – are
5) sa   – his, her 6) ses   – his, her
   ça   – that   ces   – these, those
7) de   – of, from 8) sur   – on
   deux – two   sûr   – sure, safe

(continued over)

Homonyms (cont.)

9)	vingt	– twenty	10)	se	– himself, etc.
	le vin	– wine		ce	– this, that
11)	s'est	– has	12)	la fin	– end
	c'est	– it is		la faim	– hunger
13)	(tu) es	– are	14)	(tu) as	– have
	(il) est	– is		(il) a	– has
				à	– to, at, in
15)	on	– one	16)	si	– if; so; yes
	ont	– have		six	– six
	en	– in, some etc.		la scie	– saw
17)	la mer	– sea	18)	l'heure	– hour, time
	la mère	– mother		leur	– to them; their
	le maire	– mayor		leurs	– their (pl.)
19)	mes	– my	20)	quel, etc.	– which? what?
	mais	– but			(+ *noun*)
	mai	– May		qu'elle	– that she
					(+ *verb*)
21)	s'en (aller)	– to go away	22)	sept	– seven
	cent	– hundred		cette	– this (f.)
	le sang	– blood		cet	– this (m. before vowel)
	sans	– without		c'est	– it is (as in *c'est un homme*)
23)	(il) voit	– sees	24)	le pois	– pea
	la voie	– way		le poids	– weight
	la voix	– voice		la poix	– pitch
25)	froid	– cold	26)	droit	– right, straight
	la fois	– times		le doigt	– finger
	la foi	– faith	27)	la tante	– aunt
	le foie	– liver		la tente	– tent

FAUX–AMIS

PART E

13   FAUX-AMIS

Literally meaning 'false friends', these are words which are deceptive, because, judged by their spelling or sound, they do not necessarily mean what one would expect them to mean. They make a fascinating list.

accuser	–	(also) to show
achever	–	to complete
agréer	–	to accept, to approve
aimer	–	to like, to love
arriver	–	(also) to happen, to occur
assister à	–	to attend
attendre	–	to wait for
avertir	–	to warn
balancer	–	(also) to swing
blesser	–	to wound, to injure
cacher	–	to hide, to conceal
causer	–	to chat
charger	–	(also) to load
contrôler	–	to inspect, to check
convenir	–	to suit, to agree
défendre	–	(also) to forbid, to prohibit
demander	–	to ask
demeurer	–	to live
déranger	–	to disturb
dresser	–	to raise
heurter	–	to knock against, to bump into
hisser	–	to hoist
hurler	–	to howl
ignorer	–	to be ignorant of, not to know
labourer	–	to till, to plough
lier	–	to tie
nager	–	to swim
nommer	–	(also) to appoint
partir	–	to leave, to depart
passer (un examen)	–	to sit (an exam)
poser	–	to put down
prétendre	–	to claim
ramer	–	to row

(continued over)

Faux Amis (cont.)

rapporter	–	(usually) to bring back
regarder	–	(usually) to look at
remarquer	–	(usually) to notice
rentrer	–	to return (home)
répéter	–	(also) to rehearse
replier	–	to fold up
rester	–	to stay, to remain
retirer	–	to pull out, to extract
saluer	–	(also) to greet, to wave
se servir de	–	to use
sortir	–	to go out
supplier	–	to beg, to implore
supporter	–	(usually) to suffer, to put up with
surnommer	–	to nickname
taper	–	(also) to type
traîner	–	to drag
transpirer	–	(usually) to perspire
travailler	–	to work
trier	–	to sort out, to grade
l'adresse (f)	–	(also) skill
l'apologie (f)	–	defence, justification
l'argument (m)	–	discussion, summary, outline
l'assistance (f)	–	attendance, congregation
l'avertissement	–	warning, notice
la blouse	–	(usually) overall
le bond	–	leap, bound
le bras	–	arm
la brasse	–	fathom
la bride	–	bridle, reins
la bulle	–	(usually) bubble, blister
le cabinet	–	(usually) office, room, study, surgery, closet
la cane	–	duck
le car	–	(motor) coach
la casserole	–	saucepan
la cave	–	cellar
la chair	–	flesh
la chaire	–	pulpit
le champ	–	field

la chance	–	(usually) luck
le chandelier	–	candlestick
le chat	–	cat
le chip	–	potato-crisp
la cloche	–	bell
le coin	–	corner
le collège	–	school
le conducteur	–	driver
le contrôleur	–	(usually) inspector, examiner, ticket collector
la copie	–	(also) candidate's paper
la corne	–	horn
le corps	–	(living) body
la course	–	run, race, trip, outing
la cravate	–	tie
la dent	–	tooth
la diète	–	(usually) starvation diet
le dogue	–	mastiff
l'éclair (m)	–	(usually) flash of lightning
l'essence (f)	–	(usually) petrol
l'étiquette (f)	–	(usually) label, ticket
l'évidence (f)	–	(usually) clearness
l'expérience (f)	–	(also) experiment
la fabrique	–	factory, manufacture
la farce	–	(also) practical joke, trick
la figure	–	face
la fin	–	end
la flèche	–	arrow, spire
la formation	–	(also) training
la foule	–	crowd
le four	–	oven, kiln, furnace
le front	–	(also) forehead
le gentilhomme	–	nobleman
le geste	–	gesture
la gorge	–	throat
l'habit (m)	–	coat, costume
le hasard	–	chance
l'herbe (f)	–	grass
l'hôte (f)	–	(female) guest
l'inconvénient (m)	–	disadvantage, drawback

(continued over)

Faux-Amis (cont.)

l'intelligence (f)	–	(usually) understanding, comprehension
la jalousie	–	(also) Venetian blind
la journée	–	(whole) day
le laboureur	–	ploughman
la lecture	–	reading
la librairie	–	bookshop
le magasin	–	(large) shop
la marmite	–	stewing-pot
la matinée	–	(whole) morning
le médecin	–	doctor
le membre	–	(also) limb
la messe	–	(Catholic) Mass
la mine	–	(also) appearance, look, expression, mien
la monnaie	–	(loose) change
la note	–	(also) bill, invoice, account, notice, mark
l'occasion (f)	–	opportunity, chance
l'opportunité (f)	–	opportuneness, timeliness, favourable occasion
le pain	–	bread
le pan	–	flap, shirt-tail
le pantalon	–	trousers
le parent	–	(also) relative
le pavé	–	cobblestone, paving stone
le pavement	–	ornamental tiling
la pension	–	(also) payment for board, boarding school (fees)
le pensionnaire	–	(also) boarder, resident, guest
la peste	–	(usually) plague
le pétrole	–	oil, petroleum
le photographe	–	photographer
la pièce	–	room, coin, play
la place	–	seat, town square
le plateau	–	(also) tray
le plongeur	–	(also) washer-up
la promenade	–	walk
la queue	–	(also) tail
la rate	–	spleen
le regard	–	look, gaze
les reins (m)	–	kidneys
la répétition	–	(also) rehearsal
les restes (m)	–	remains

la ride	–	wrinkle
le roman	–	novel
le sable	–	sand
la serviette	–	(also) towel, briefcase
le siège	–	(also) seat
le singe	–	monkey
le slip	–	(under)pants
le smoking	–	dinner-jacket
le stage	–	course, probationary period
le sud	–	south
le talon	–	(usually) heel
le timbre	–	postage stamp
la toilette	–	wash(ing), dressing, getting ready; washstand
le tour	–	(also) turn, trick
la tour	–	tower, rook (chess)
le travail	–	work
les vacances (f)	–	holidays, vacation
le vague	–	vagueness
la vague	–	wave
la vase	–	(river) mud
le verger	–	orchard
le vers	–	line (of poetry)
la veste	–	jacket
le veston	–	jacket
les waters (m)	–	toilet
actuel	–	of the present day, current
actuellement	–	at present, at the moment
ancien	–	(also) former, ex-
blanc	–	white
blessé	–	wounded, injured
brave	–	(also) good, honest, worthy
car	–	for
en train de	–	engaged in, in the process of
fatal	–	(also) fateful, inevitable
génial	–	brilliant, inspired
gentil	–	kind, nice
inhabité	–	uninhabited
joli	–	pretty

(continued over)

Faux-Amis (cont.)

laid	–	ugly
large	–	wide
merci	–	thank you
mince	–	thin
or	–	now, well
pour	–	for, in order to
sensible	–	sensitive
surnommé	–	nicknamed
sympathique	–	(usually) likeable, pleasant
unique	–	only, single, sole
usé	–	worn out, shabby
vilain	–	mean, ugly, wicked

PART F

14   ESSAY WRITING

(1)   *DO* write *simple* French *correctly.*

(2)   *DO* try to think in French as much as possible.

(3)   *DO* think of phrases, idioms, etc., which you have seen previously, and incorporate them *if relevant* into your essay.

(4)   *DO* pay careful attention to *spelling, agreements, accents, number and gender.*

(5)   *DO* use all the information available in a guided essay,
i.e. listen carefully to readings, and make use of any questions beneath pictures from the point of grammar, spelling etc.

(1)   *DO NOT* think of a *sophisticated* English sentence, and attempt to translate word for word.

(2)   *DO NOT* translate a phrase one word at a time, but try to think what the French would say.

(3)   *DO NOT* write more than is necessary, if this is at the expense of accuracy.

Verbs ending in -oir and -oire (except voir, s'asseoir)

U group

Vouloir

Je voul*us*   –   *I wanted*
Tu voul*us*
Il voul*ut*
Nous voul*ûmes*
Vous voul*ûtes*
Ils voul*urent*

Irregular Verbs

The *passé simple* can often be formed from the *past participle* of the verb in question, e.g.

avoir	→ j'ai *eu*	→	j'*eus*
dire	→ j'ai *dit*	→	je *dis*
prendre	→ j'ai *pris*	→	je *pris*

Common Exceptions

être (to be)	→ je fus
faire (to make, to do)	→ je fis
écrire (to write)	→ j'écrivis
couvrir (to cover)	→ je couvris
ouvrir (to open)	→ j'ouvris
souffrir (to suffer)	→ je souffris
offrir (to offer)	→ j'offris
naître (to be born)	→ je naquis
vaincre (to conquer)	→ je vainquis
voir (to see)	→ je vis
mourir (to die)	→ je mourus
venir (to come)	→ je vins
tenir (to hold)	→ je tins

16.2   Past Anterior Tense
(le passé antérieur)

(1)   The *past anterior* is a *compound* tense.
(2)   Its use is confined basically to *written* French.
(3)   It is equivalent to the English *pluperfect*.
(4)   It is used in subordinate clauses after certain temporal conjunctions when one action is immediately followed by a second in the past tense.
(5)   The main clause must be in the *past historic*.

Conjunctions

quand ⎫
lorsque ⎬   when

aussitôt que ⎫
dès que ⎬   as soon as

après que   after

N.B.   It is also used after the adverb *à peine . . . que* scarcely . . . than, which requires inversion of subject and verb.

Equation

Past Historic of *avoir* or *être* + past participle = Past Anterior,

e.g.   J'eus vendu – I had sold.
        Il eut dit – he had said.
        Nous fûmes arrivés – we had arrived.

Use of the past anterior

Quand ils *eurent préparé* leur pique-nique, ils *partirent*.
When they *had prepared* their picnic, they *set off*.

Aussitôt qu'elle *fut arrivée*, elle *s'assit*.
As soon as she *had arrived*, she *sat down*.

16.3 Subjunctive Mood
(le subjonctif)

(1) The subjunctive mood is used comparatively rarely in French to state suppositions rather than facts (indicative mood).

(2) It is equivalent to the English *if I were you; God bless you; if this be true.* etc.

(3) It is used after:
  (a) Verbs which express desire,
  (b) Verbs which express emotion,
  (c) Verbs which express uncertainty,
  (d) A superlative expression,
  (e) An impersonal verb or expression,
  (f) Certain adverbial conjunctions.

(4) In general there is a toning down of certainty or likelihood.

(5) The subjunctive has four tenses in French, the *present, imperfect, perfect* and *pluperfect*. The *present* tense is certainly the most important of the four tenses.

16.4 Formation of the Present Subjunctive
(le présent du subjonctif)

General Rule

Remove the *-nt* from the 3rd person plural Present Tense, to get the 1st person singular of the Present Subjunctive.

e.g.	attendre	ils attende*nt*	j'attende
	boire	ils boive*nt*	je boive

Remove the *-ons* from the 1st person plural Present tense to get the stem of the 1st and 2nd plural Present Subjunctive.

e.g.	boire	nous buv*ons*	nous buv*ions*
	jeter	nous jet*ons*	nous jet*ions*

Endings

-e, -es, -e, -ions, -iez, -ent, **e.g.**:

Finir	**Prendre**	**Voir**
Je finis*se*	Je prenn*e*	Je voi*e*
Tu finis*ses*	Tu prenn*es*	Tu voi*es*
Il finis*se*	Il prenn*e*	Il voi*e*
Nous finiss*ions*	Nous pren*ions*	Nous voy*ions*
Vous finiss*iez*	Vous pren*iez*	Vous voy*iez*
Ils finiss*ent*	Ils prenn*ent*	Ils voi*ent*

Important Exceptions

Être	**Avoir**	**Aller**
Je sois	J'aie	J'aille
Tu sois	Tu aies	Tu ailles
Il soit	Il ait	Il aille
Nous soyons	Nous ayons	Nous allions
Vous soyez	Vous ayez	Vous alliez
Ils soient	Ils aient	Ils aillent

Faire	**Pouvoir**	**Vouloir**
Je fasse	Je puisse	Je veuille
Tu fasses	Tu puisses	Tu veuilles
Il fasse	Il puisse	Il veuille
Nous fassions	Nous puissions	Nous voulions
Vous fassiez	Vous puissiez	Vous vouliez
Ils fassent	Ils puissent	Ils veuillent

Note Also:

Savoir	→	Je sache, etc.
Pleuvoir	→	Il pleuve
Falloir	→	Il faille

16.5 Uses of the Subjunctive

It is used after the following:

vouloir que . . .	to wish that	*desire*
regretter que . . .	to regret that	
c'est dommage que . . .	it is a pity that	*emotion*
être content que . . .	to be pleased that	
avoir peur que . . . ne (+ subj. verb)	to be afraid that	
je ne crois pas que . . .	I don't think that	*uncertainty*
croyez-vous que . . . ?	do you think that?	
il est possible que . . .	it is possible that	*impersonal*
il est impossible que . . .	it is impossible that	*expressions*
il faut que . . .	you must	
quoique bien que	although	
pour que afin que	in order that so that	*Adverbial* *conjunctions*
sans que	without	
avant que	before	
jusqu' à ce que	until	
(attendre que *to wait until*)		
à moins que . . . ne (+ subj. verb)	unless	

17 Answers to Quiz

(1) oiseau
(2) cinq; coq
(3) six; dix
(4) second(e); secondaire
(5) oeil (pl. les yeux)
(6) onze (e.g. le onze mai)
(7) créée

18   GLOSSARY

An explanation of some of the grammatical terms used in this book

Direct object:

A noun or pronoun which directly receives the action of the verb,

e.g.   Je vois *l'homme* – I see *the man*

Je *le* vois – I see *him*

Indirect object:

A noun or pronoun which indirectly receives the action of the verb,

e.g.   Je *lui* donne le livre – I give the book *to him*

I give *him* the book

Reflexive object:

A pronoun which refers back to the subject of the sentence,

e.g.   Je *me* lave – I wash *(myself)*

Disjunctive pronoun:

A strong pronoun, i.e. one which is not attached to a verb in such a way as to have a direct grammatical relationship with it,

e.g.   Qui a ouvert la porte? *Lui*? Non, *elle.*

Who opened the door? Did he? No, she did.

(contrast conjunctive or weak pronouns)

Present Participle:

The form of the verb which ends in 'ant' in French and 'ing' in English,

e.g.   donnant – giving.

Imperative Mood:

The command form of the verb (from Latin *impero* – I command),

e.g.   lève-toi!; levez-vous! – stand up!

Subjunctive Mood:

A form of the verb used when the content of the clause is being doubted, supposed, wished or thought, rather than asserted,

e.g.   Je souhaite que tu viennes pendant les vacances de Pâques,

I wish you would come during the Easter holidays.